Boci's New Shoes

Austine Royer Smith

BOCI'S NEW SHOES

ISBN-13: Paperback: 978-1-64151-873-4

Printed in the United States of America

LitFire
PUBLISHING

LitFire LLC
1-800-511-9787
www.litfirepublishing.com
order@litfirepublishing.com

It is with deep appreciation that I dedicate this miracle book to the Vacation Bible School children who gave their offerings and supplies to the children of Haiti. These children attended Bible school at:

Abundant Life Fellowship Church
Altus, Arkansas

Bloomingdale Christian Alliance Church
Bloomingdale, Georgia

First Baptist Church Garden City, Georgia

Sand Hill Baptist Church Guyton, Georgia

This is a true story of a Haitian boy named Boci. Boci lives in the high mountains of Thiotte, Haiti with his mother and sister.

Boci and his family live in a mud and grass hut like most Haitians.

Boci and his family speaks Creole but it is easy to understand what he tries to tell you.

Boci's mother has to cook their food on the outside because of the heat and danger of the hut catching on fire. Their one meal of the day is rice and sometimes mixed with beans.

Boci and his family are very poor like most Haitians. Everyday Boci has to go into the village and beg for food.

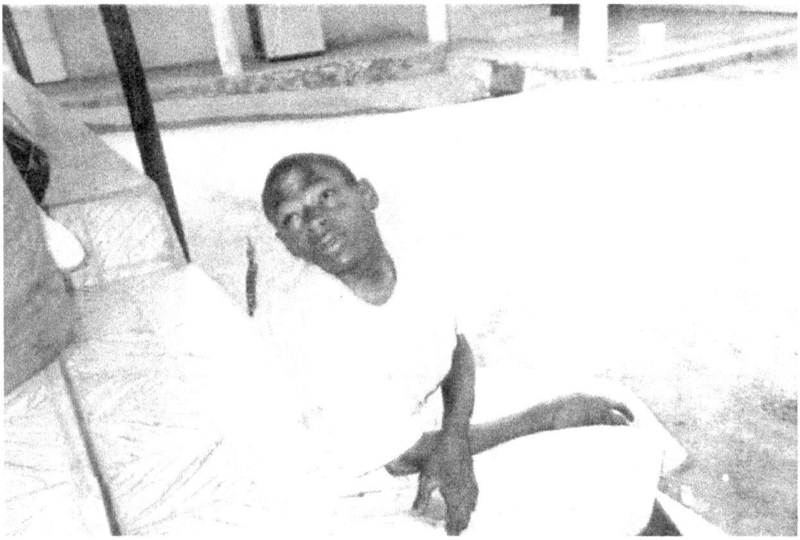

It is very difficult for Boci to do physical work because he was born with a severe affliction. Boci is very hunched backed and dwarfed. Boci became a target for people to "bully" him and mistreat him so very cruelly. Boci cannot defend himself so he tries to laugh it off and be kind to teasers.

One summer a huge hurricane came to the area and caused rock slides and mud slides. Whole villages were covered completely with the rock and mud. The rutty roads had become impossible to travel on. Only people who had donkies and burros could travel.

Sister Austine. a missionary, brought a medical team to help the sick and wounded people of Thiotte. Sister Austine and the team held a clinic on the front porch of the house that they were staying in.

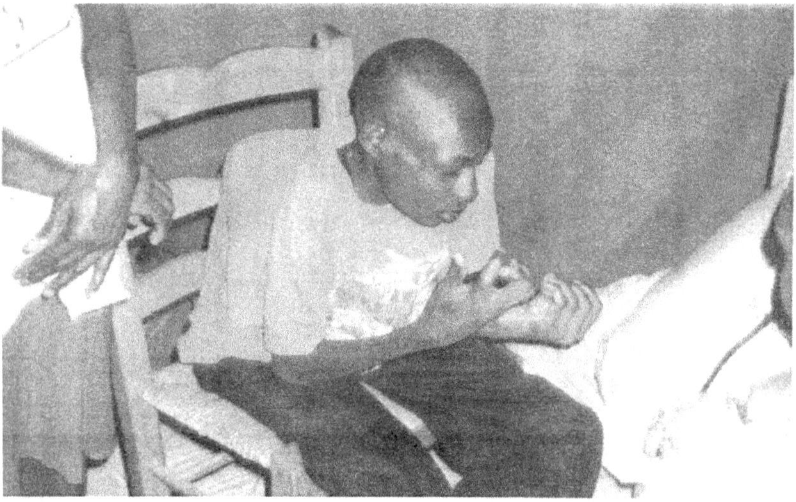

Boci came to the "front porch" clinic and the medical team gave him a good physical examination. The doctor gave him some medicine, vitamins, food and clothes.

Boci was very happy and called the missionary his "Amie" (friend.)

After several more trips to the village. Sister Austine took Boci to church with her. Boci was very happy and he sat and listened to Sister Austine speaking to the people through an interpreter about how Jesus loves us and cares for them.

Sister Austine promised Boci that if he would go to church every Sunday until she got back to Thiotte in two months that she would bring him a new pair of "church shoes." Sister Austine drew an outline of Boci's feet so she could get the right size.

The next day Sister Austine returned back home and was very sad because she had left the drawing of Boci's feet in Haiti. But when she got to her house, there was a big black trash bag sitting beside her front door and in the top of the bag was a new pair of black shining shoes just Boci's size.

Sister Austine was so happy because she knew that God had answered Boci's prayer for a new pair of shoes and she knew that Boci was going to church.

In two months sister Austine and the team went back to the village and Boci saw the mission truck coming into the village. Boci began running and yelling “Eglise, Eglise” (which is church in his language.)

He was trying to tell Sister Austine that he had been to church every Sunday and he added “mama too!”

After arriving at the mission house and unloading the supplies, Boci was presented his new shoes and told how God had answered his prayers with a miracle for being faithful. Boci had never had shoes before. Only ragged flip flops. The shoes fit perfectly. Everyone was happy. Boci started yelling "J'AIM VOUS", "J AIM VOUS" (I LOVE YOU. I LOVE YOU.) "DIEU REPOND MOI DIEU REPOND MOI" (GOD ANSWERED MY PRAYER.)

When Sister Austine and the team started to leave the village she told Boci she was going to send him to school. Now he had a school uniform, Bible, backpack, supplies and of course new black shoes. Sister Austine hugged him and showed him how to say "I love you" with his hand.

We still do not know "who" left the big black bag with the miracle shoes in it!!

Other books by the missionary are available by donations only to:

Austine Royer Smith
Foundling House Mission
P. O. Box 18114
Garden City. Georgia 31418

All funds from these books will go to:

The Foundling House Mission

HAITI IS WAITING	$5.50
IF THAT ISN'T LOVE	$6.00
THE EDGE OF THE FIELD	$7.95
PRESENT BOUQUETS	$11.32
BOCI'S NEW SHOES	$5.49
GRANDMA WAVES WITH HER HEART	$9.99
SHIPPING PER BOOK	$1.30

For speaking engagements or information about mission teams contact:

Austine Royer Smith at the address above or
austinersmith@aol.com

CPSIA information can be obtained
at www.ICGtesting.com
Printed in the USA
BVHW030925020322
630411BV00032B/81

9 781641 518734